LATE STARTER

ROBERT FERGUSON

authorHOUSE®

AuthorHouse™ UK
1663 Liberty Drive
Bloomington, IN 47403 USA
www.authorhouse.co.uk
Phone: 0800.197.4150

© 2018 Robert Ferguson. All rights reserved.

No part of this book may be reproduced, stored in a retrieval system, or transmitted by any means without the written permission of the author.

Published by AuthorHouse 03/19/2018

ISBN: 978-1-5462-8967-8 (sc)
ISBN: 978-1-5462-8966-1 (hc)
ISBN: 978-1-5462-8965-4 (e)

Print information available on the last page.

Any people depicted in stock imagery provided by Getty Images are models, and such images are being used for illustrative purposes only.
Certain stock imagery © Getty Images.

This book is printed on acid-free paper.

Because of the dynamic nature of the Internet, any web addresses or links contained in this book may have changed since publication and may no longer be valid. The views expressed in this work are solely those of the author and do not necessarily reflect the views of the publisher, and the publisher hereby disclaims any responsibility for them.

Scripture quotations marked NRSV are taken from the New Revised Standard Version of the Bible, Copyright © 1989, by the Division of Christian Education of the National Council of the Churches of Christ in the United States of America. Used by permission. All rights reserved.

Scripture quotations marked NIV are taken from the Holy Bible, New International Version®. NIV®. Copyright © 1973, 1978, 1984 by International Bible Society. Used by permission of Zondervan. All rights reserved. [Biblica]

Scripture quotations marked KJV are from the Holy Bible, King James Version (Authorized Version). First published in 1611. Quoted from the KJV Classic Reference Bible, Copyright © 1983 by The Zondervan Corporation.

Contents

Introduction ix

I. Red Flares and Other Events 1

Red Flares 3
Caught In The Hills 5
Violets 6
Ritual: Penn Hill 7
Overture And Beginners 8
Flamenco 9
Sun, Shade And Cyclamen 11
School Matinee 12
Nefusa, 1967 13
Many Reluctant Returns 17
Sequential Life 19
Mr. Hughes' Removal Van 20
Interior Decoration 21
The Cottage By The Golf Course 22
Sealers 23
Sonnet To An Old-Fashioned Librarian 24
At The Marriage Of 25
Beached People 26
Fireworks 28
That Hand At Table 29
A Childhood Garden In Kent 30
Into Care 31
Aleppo, 2016 32

II. Characters Known & Unknown 35

The Old Toby-Jug Maker 37
Rembrandt – Self-Portraits 39
Councillor Carter 41

Working From Home 43
Moving House 44
What Does She Do? 45
My Grandpa's Beard 47
Buttons 48
Welsh Row, Beam Street 49
Views Across The Tyne 50
The Bear's Spring 51
Heritage 53
Autumn 54
Weekend Neighbours 55
The Expert 56
No "Click-And-Drop" For Me! 57
Love Is Not Everything 58
Next Door 59
Caravaggio 60
Spring In A Winter Place 61
Valentine For A Long-Standing Relationship 63
Khrushchev's Shoe 64
The Engineer And The Poet 65
What Do You Make? 66
Martyred By Lions 68
Victim's Possessions 69
The English Mystery 70

III.   Cats & Other Creatures 73

Sunny 75
The Visiting Dragon 76
Cat, Dreaming 77
Sonnet Of New Life 78
Steps 79
Prejudices And Realities 80
Bought At The Sales 81
Gabble-Gobble 82
Owl 84
In Pusscat's Power 86

IV. Soul Poems 87

Midnight Sparrow 89
Fatherhood 91
And The Cars Went By 92
Christmas, Here And Now 94
Coincidences? 96
You Are The Other 97
Questions 98
Doubt And Faith 99
The Solution Was There All The Time! 100
Where Is It, And What Is It For? 102
Wakefulness 103
Diver 104
Lidded Pots 105
Sunday 106
To A Monastery Guesthouse 107
Merton 108
Eight Stones 110
Sunrise, On May-Morning 111
Creation 112
Abandoned 113
Cathedral Close 114
The Last Task 115
Funeral, And Beyond 116
And Next ..? 118

Index Of Titles 119
Index Of First Lines 123

Introduction

I was brought up in a home and school of traditional English culture in the 1950's. Together with the strict musical disciplines of cathedral choristership, these influences encouraged and inculcated an early appreciation of classical English poetry – Chaucer in Coghill's bouncing translation as well as the original author's fascinating French/Italian 13th Century English, Shakespeare, Shelley, Colleridge, Wordsworth and their peers – and of the beauty of 16th Century Church-Latin in the anthems of Thomas Tallis and William Byrd and the rhythmic poetry of the King James' version of the Bible. Inevitably, these influences left indelible marks in the working of mind, memory and inherent taste.

Early poems appreciative of pretty girls were giggled-over embarrassingly by the recipients and their friends, and my only school prize came from the annual poetry competition in which mine was the sole entry (it was a somewhat macho school); and then university, work and family intervened, and I wrote only for others, the formal prose of academic papers, business proposals and reports, briefings and statements, and letters in measured terms to the better newspapers. Perhaps this, too, had its effect, for I am aware that my poetry is not obscure, or at least is intended not to be so. Decades of being required habitually to seek clarity in written communication has been added to a nature impatient with writings from which the reader is required to chisel the author's meaning or motivation from the obscurity either of convolution or of minimalist three-word lines.

After some thirty-odd years of intense work, responsibility and travel, I collapsed. Perhaps frustration had something to do with it? Not being able to do what I was meant to do? Who knows? For some months, I was too exhausted to be concerned that no clear diagnosis was ever offered. While eventually beginning to recover, however, I began to paint, deepened my knowledge of theology, and took up the daily duties of sacristan in our local parish church, until cancer struck both my wife and myself.

No longer capable of looking after ourselves, we moved into a care home, where I led and wrote for a Poetry Group of residents, from which much of the content of this collection arose. When my wife died, I moved out of the care home to resume the quiet of independent life, rebuild a support-network of friends old and new, and begin to consider, expand and organise the material that follows.

The book is in four sections. Each could make a separate pamphlet, if I were confident that I had time to arrange and publish them in that form. But I am not, so they are (almost) all here, and the individual reader will inevitably find more to interest them in one section than another.

The first section, 'Red Flares and other events', is characterised by actions, and the emotions to which they give rise. Some of the poems are drawn from my travels in Europe, North Africa and the various regions of the U.K., others from various stages of family life, a few simply from travels of the affections. Throughout my life, the calming effect of empty landscapes - fields, fens, woodlands, mountains, deserts – has been a great comfort to me, as is from time to time illustrated here.

'Characters Known and Unknown', the second section, reflects, sometimes more lightly, on people observed, admired, imagined, or met, and on my own memories of a life lived in a number of different places, conditions and physical and cultural environments. People are repeatedly fascinating. So many of them share our own ways and values, and as often differ from us in ways we find interesting, if difficult to understand.

Animals have been a source of fascination and affection all my life, cats most of all. Hence the third section, 'Cats and Other Creatures', is very special to me. There were cats at home in my childhood, and a sequence of very individual cats in our homes in various places at various times. In the care home to which we had to resort eventually, we were appointed the carers of the house pet, a rescue cat of advanced years when she came to us, who used to sit upright on my knee in an evening and watch the television with great concentration. Her passing made a deep and lasting wound in my heart, the still-incomplete healing of which was much assisted by the chef's cat, Sunny, featured here, though he was neither permitted, nor appeared to want, to come indoors.

And there are other creatures in this section of the book, too, all but one gentle, dignified, beautiful, and loved for simply existing to smooth the sharp corners of the world we share with them.

The fourth and final section presents matters of soul and faith, mostly but not exclusively Christian. It begins with the Christmas mystery and culminates in the mysteries of death and the Beyond. Many of these poems were written for, and circulated among, friends in our local Church of England parish after my retirement, and in our care home where, in the absence of any other spiritual activity when we arrived, I led a brief service of worship each Sunday morning, attended by residents and carers of various Christian denominations and of other religions from across the world. By definition, there can be only one Creator God,. We choose to worship Him in different ways, usually according to upbringing and habit. If we are wrong, He – or She - will forgive.

The commonality that binds the sections together is the memory of experiences - not exclusively mine, for several of these poems were stimulated by stories that others have told me of their lives, or by events reported in the news to be occurring beyond the range of my own immediate experience. Many, under the stimulus of such origins, are total fictions, fancies, whimsies. That is an author's privilege. But several of them grew from feelings, often deep feelings, about the rightness, wrongness, justice, love and ridiculousness of what had happened around me, at first-hand or second-hand, or indeed what I myself had sometimes done.

Why does a poet publish what is almost always very personal work? Pride in a small degree of technical achievement? I fear yes, though I hope that has not been my primary motivation. Far more powerful seems to be the innately human need to communicate, to say what we see and feel, what moves our hearts and fears, what our minds perceive as sufficiently important to us as to require being offered for others to share, hopefully for their benefit. We publish, often, perhaps, so that someone else will weep or laugh with us, be caused to stop their world and review it, and perhaps be different afterwards.

Robert Ferguson
Spring, 2018.

I

RED FLARES AND OTHER EVENTS

Red Flares

White sails when they left, all those months ago,
From this same harbour, wreathed tonight in dusk
And rain, and the gale blowing fit to bust
Through the cliff itself around the bay,
And the harbour lights upon the pier-heads
Utterly blotted out by sheets of spray.
But it *is* their hull, pale blue once, pitch black now
In the dark and muck of a long voyage,
And their short mast aft.
   But where's the jib-boom
     That jutted proud at the bow? And the main,
     Broken off now at the lower cross-trees,
        And the stays sagging to port when the wind allows?
And there's her red flare! They're in trouble now,
Knowing this tack won't make the harbour mouth,
And no sea-room to try a second time.

And there's the lifeboat siren, and the feet
Of crewmen running for their oilskin gear,
Life-jackets, rubber boots, leaping to their places
As the boat begins to slide, to race down
And disappear, it seems, in towering foam
Just as the engine roars, screws turn, and up
She rears, and rolls towards the sea again.
And another red flare rises, further out.

And morning now. The storm past, little knots
Of sombre faces gathered on the quay.
Low tide now, so, beneath the cliff, they see
What scraps and fragments, timber, wires and spars,
Remain. The lifeboat picked up two last night,
The other being found at dawn, caught up
On a lobster-pot, set by Jem Hankins
Where he always does, in the next-door bay.

We brought them to the church which was their home.
All three were christened there, and there they'll lie.
They'd been away so long, so keen to see
Their Mums and Dads and Aunts and friends again.
They couldn't wait, stand off in one more storm
After all the others they had known. Now
They were nearly home. They knew the sea here,
They could make it.

    But they didn't, did they?

Faces fade in time. On my mind's eye, though,
There will always be two fireworks, red, red,
"Help!" Too late for them. Always there for me.

Caught In The Hills

A night-walk on the limestone hills,
'Neath cold, clear sky and stars a-bright.
You'll see for miles, beyond the coast,
Believe the world could never end.

Then, by the morning, silently,
A surreptitious, alien sheet
Has filled your valleys, climbed your hills,
And all your world has disappeared.

Who is there here but you and I?
What is that shape? Where is the path
That might lead home, secure and safe,
Not scuff and slide our feet away?

Sit down and wait. The rock is damp,
But better here than hurt below.
The warming flask, the heartening cake,
The damp, the grey's uncertainty.

Baaaa. Bleeet. We hear <u>and</u> see. It moves,
Becoming real again. A bush,
A wall, the thinning murk, the sun
At last, a disk of yellow gold.

    All's well. It's time to gather up and go.

Violets

One afternoon in Spring, O best beloved,
We dressed you in your padded, pale blue suit,
Which covered you from toes to high-peaked hood,
And took your reins to give you every freedom,
And a light picnic – always a picnic, for your darling Mum –
And loaded up the car and climbed the Hills
Into the dappled woodland, truly dappled
(No other word for it, with the sun's bright stipples
Edging between the hazel leaves and branches)
And we let you run, on your reins, we running on behind you
Into the dark green / rich blue violets
That littered – literally littered – the clearings' floors,
And scattered sunlight, in a way magical.

And do those clearings still exist today?
Are Devon woods, and Devon violets still
Wild, and wide open? Can a little child
Still run and trip and fall, and gurgle up,
        Laughing and grinning,
From the wonderous flowers and scents that gave you so much pleasure
    All those years ago?

Ritual: Penn Hill

It was a ritual, nothing more than that,
    It did what rituals do,
        It reminded,
Marked the passage of time, no more.

And yet, we did it every New Year's Day.
    Parents and children,
        Uncles, cousins, aunts,
We met to climb Penn Hill, and smell the wind.

It isn't especially high, or cragged, or hard
    To climb, whatever age we be,
        And, in the frost,
The thistle's prick is muted by the clean, cold air.

From at the top, there is a view, of course,
    Over the valley, over the city roofs,
        Abbey and Bridge,
Assembly Rooms and spire, and cranes and river.

But everyone has seen that view before.
    That isn't why we did it. Nor to see
        If toboggan-snow
Had yet arrived. We'd see that from indoors.

No, we climbed up for New Year, to give thanks
That we had made it through the last twelve months,
    Look forward to the next,
Remember those who've gone before us,
        Into rest and peace.

Overture And Beginners

Stage dark and theatre still, strings set the theme.
Dimmed spot on centre-stage, a folded figure,
Pale and pink, submissive and subdued.

Back left, a dim green light, low down
Illuminates tree-trunks, darker figures, men
Creeping as if in danger through the trees,
Coming from distance, tiny, careful steps.

Back right, a pale light, sun on snow, perhaps,
An open landscape, steppes. Some figures, small,
Peasants expelled and dispossessed, approach
In a tight band for safety, edging past
The threatening forest.

        Brass expands, then horns
And trumpets grow their own proud voice, and powerful men
And stronger lights approach behind the peasants,
Who withdraw into wing-shadows. "Look, it is the King!"
Though no voice says it.

Spot increases, folded figure stands,
Unfolding, stretching up, and bowing low
Before the advancing power. But who will take her,
Who will make her dance? For what?
For freedom, or for patriarchal power?
Who are the shadows, deep within the trees,
As yet unseen, but with a part to play.

The drama holds us, music, movement. Time
Is neither now nor here. All is bewitching,
And bewitched, for a few hours in which
We live a different life, a life not ours.

Flamenco

In pitch darkness, we groped for a seat,
Or a cushion on the edge of a step would do,
Past knees, on toes, with apologies,
Hand-in-hand for fear of separation,
To squash in between two people –
Men, women? - no-one seemed to care.

Then gradually, dim light, like the dawn in winter,
From one bulb, and we could just see
A figure near-crouched on a chair in a corner,
Arms grasping bright wood that reflected its polish
And strings. And he sat quite still.

For silent, and centred, another tall figure appeared,
Dark, shadowed, except for the top of her nose
        And amazing sharp cheek-bones,
                and castanetted hands
Stretching up to the sky as if each were a pointer
To a spirit that hovered in the dark of the room.

Black lace on her shoulders, black hair on her head,
And a black comb, jet black, standing up high and proud.
Black skirt to her ankles, and black shoes whose heels
Started the movement. Their tips beat a rhythm,
First very quietly, but as they accelerated,
Louder and louder and louder they went.

Then she screamed! It was song, but a primitive sound,
From a folk who had suffered, whose land and whose homes
Had been taken.
              And she swirled
As her shoes beat the wood floor again and again and again.

In less than hour, it was finished, but we
Like the dancer and player, exhausted,
Could no more have moved in the on-going darkness
Than we could have done what they'd done there before us.
Exhausted in spirit, rent, spitted by passion,
We gradually staggered away from that focus
While never forgetting what we had felt.

Sun, Shade And Cyclamen

(Seville, Andalucia)

Opposite the Cathedral, beneath the Giralda tower,
Across the street, beyond the carriages,
An alley opens, tunnel-like, pitch dark.
High buildings' shadows make the tourist cower,
But the narrow pavement leads one on,
Deeper and deeper, seemingly, until,
Without a warning, house-fronts painted white
Open into sunshine blinding-bright,
With windows, shuttered tight against the sun,
Outlined by delicately painted tiles,
Their balconies hung heavily with flowers.
Flowers in tight bunches, multi-coloured, wave
And crowd in masses, hanging through the bars
Like young girls' dresses, layered and frilled, for show
In the wide plaza opening up below.

School Matinee

Like ancient armies gathering for battle
The pupil columns come,
Emptying the charabancs, stumbling to the front,
Knots and groups, in pairs, alone,
With bags, without, with cardigans, in uniform or not,
Shambling and walking, excited, quiet, texting,
Shouting, mumbling, gossiping, and silent, wide-eyed, puzzling.

The doors are breached, the foyer filled, the hills of stairs assaulted,
The seats will bang, the noise will rise,
A storm of voices, cut by darkness, expectation-tensed, as curtains part,
And silence, broken by one voice:

"Who's there?" "Nay, answer me, and unfold yourself."
    "Bernardo?" "He".
The words well-known – or not – from desks and scripts
    In schools throughout the land,
All brought in myriad minds to honour Stratford and her son.

Nefusa, 1967

A hundred miles south from Tarabulus,
Nefusa's cliff rises a thousand feet
Straight from the plain cut by the sea and covered by its sand.
Where Roman legions drilled beside the waves,
Built columned temples, colonnaded squares,
Modern soldiers' columns shamble,
Seeking a war they cannot join,
Pretending to know which way to march, for want
Of maps and guns and hats and everything.

Oilmen and families panic. Huge cargo planes
Sweep in and out to extricate them, while
Giving rise only to rumours of bombing raids.

On the escarpment, village kids from one continent
Have been settled for months to teach more village kids
The international language of the modern world's
Air travel and communication, trade and song.
Peacefolk bring peace by their example, and their gift
Of time and love, and chalk and pen and ink
Pushed left to right, as opposites in so many aspects meet.

Now and then, the Wanderer parks a car
Covered in dust, tyres worn, outside their house,
And she cooks more of what she has –
Cous-cous and peppers, eggs and maybe goat -
To share another plate. It makes a change
From pre-cooked curry, heated on a stove
Wedged in the back of the Wanderer's bedroom-car.

But, with the Wanderer far to the North and safe,
Word comes of war which hits the local pride.
Peacefolk become the only target here
For huge frustrations in the people left behind
From fighting for their brothers' lives and homes;
And Peacefolk are cut off: no car, no 'phone,
No 'plane to lift them out and back to home.

Back in the city, bosses, asked for news,
Have none. "Won't you go out and get them?"
"No! What a risk!" "I'll go,"
The Wanderer volunteers. "Give me a car."
Much consultation. Daren't they risk a car?
Finally, "Yes, but on your own, you know."

Through early morning cyclists in their hordes,
Hostile to someone of the enemy race,
In a huge, alien van with strange controls,
Essential handles and sticks in hidden places,
Meaningless dials he's never seen before,
The Wanderer threads his way out of the town,
Dreading a forced stop with only a general pass
Which may or may not pass muster. He can't know
Whether it says this man is friend or foe.

Onto the plain at last, with friendly dunes
He has admired so often previously.
The cliff's in sight. The sweeping, swirling road
Climbs cuttingly across its front. And then,
Across the road a barrier, and shed. A soldier squats,
Chewing, beside the road, but even so,
It's the feared checkpoint. Changing down to stop.

A greeting. Grins. A handshake. (Sweat.) But,
The soldier's on his feet, now, hand outstretched
For something inexplicable. Time to test
The general *laiser passer*. Hand it out.
Praise be, the soldier holds it upside down,
As puzzled by its writing as its source.
Instructs (presumably, "Wait here") and goes
Into the hut. An officer appears – and he can read!

Questions. A shrug. More questions, pointing.
"Gharyan," the Wanderer says, for that is where
The road leads. Where else would he go?
Tired, hot and nothing threatened by one man
In one old, dusty, dirty, tatty van,
The officer shouts a word, the barrier moves,
The pass is handed back, the clutch engaged,
The van advances slowly to the hill,
And up, and on.
    "What next?" the Wanderer thinks.

Atop the cliff, the village. Not a soul in sight
Until, before the Peacefolk's small square house,
An angry, screaming, shrieking, hating crowd,
Fists waving, truly a lynch-mob, calling Peacefolk out.
No chance for calm. Negotiating's out.
"Parp, parp" the van-horn loudly. "Here I come.
Get ready, Peacefolk, this is your get-out."
Back up the van into and through the crowd.
Ignore the thumps on the van's sides.
Assume the crowd will move away
As we creep back, though Heaven help us all
If someone won't.

They do. The van is stopped its rear-doors' width
From Peacefolk's front door. Lock the van from inside
And run back to throw the rear doors open just like shields.

Peacefolk appear, a case is thrown by each into the van.
They follow. Doors locked. Engine revved. Creep out.
The crowd falls back. Don't meet their eyes. Don't stop.
On the road now, out of their village home
Where they have given love and received fear
Far, far beyond what they could have foreseen
In their own continent. Relax, now, both,
But only 'till we face the check-point at the bottom of the cliff....
Will we get past it?

And, when they reach it, look, it isn't there!
It's been withdrawn, within this last, short hour!

Back to the city now, and some safety.
Discharge the rescued, and return the van,
    And hear of none of them ever again.

Many Reluctant Returns

Inside the case of my Grandfather's grandfather clock,
Beneath the dial with its painted moon and stars,
Behind the glass door, shining gloomily,
Swung the pendulum, heavy, metallic, gold.
    Tick, it went, now and then.
            Tock.
Then tick again, after a while. Its character
   Was peaceful, inevitable, calming,
      Friendly,
         There.

I grew up with that clock beside me,
Beside the chair with thick, tall arms and back,
So large no-one could see me when I burrowed down with a book,
    Except the clock.
He knew I was there, or not there, actually,
Deep through the far side of my book,
Deep through the distance into the country,
Far away, over the ocean, under wide sails,
On different continents, or an island beach beneath palm trees.
And the clock chimed.
       Every quarter, a single Ding,
       Every half a double Ding-Dong,
       Every hour, a cacophony of Binging and Banging
That you thought would never, ever, end!
But it helped you to know where you should be.

It called me back from my mountain, or valley, or tree-house
Which would never fit into Grandfather's tiny yard;
But I'd been there, in my chair, with his clock,
   And now I could return, calmly, peacefully,
      Without undue effort or demand.

Now with their telephones, texting and mailing,
Now with their cameras and digital timepieces
All built into their life-style devices,
All of them driving the children immediately
From one thing to the next in a rush,
Will they have time to enjoy a brief journey,
      Imaginatively,
And return reluctantly, as I did,
      At the call of a gentle friend?

Sequential Life

In Spring, we watched them, bare but hazy green
As the buds formed and grew from matt to sheen,
And burst out, leaf on leaf and yet more leaves,
Until they stood out proud like early sheaves
Of hand-mown grass in meadows in the sky.

In a good summer, there they hang above
Where rugs and picnics claim their welcome shade
And honeyed bodies move round with the sun,
Appreciating nothing of their gift
Of cool refreshment from distracting rays.

Good summers, without rain, will make them dry,
And green will turn to yellow by and by,
And then to rotted, crumbled, powdered-edged
Destruction, dropped on fields that are bare-hedged
To feed the worms, renew the soil again.

And through the winter, 'neath the snow and ice,
Between the ditches seeking to suffice
The acquifers for next year's crop, the trees
Wait dormant for the food that they will seize
By their roots, and raise to topmost twigs

For Spring to warm and make into the buds
Which, in a few months more, will signal life.

Mr. Hughes' Removal Van

"He's here, he's here." "What, now?" "Yes,
      Drawing up outside."
"You sure it's him?" "It's big enough. You'd get the house inside."
"But I'm not ready. There's these cups, and Auntie's vases, too.
"Oh, leave *them*, at least. They don't mean much to you."
"They DO." "I've always hated them."
      "Good morning, all. It's Hughes.
Are we all ready then, to start to load the van?
"Oh, Mr. Hughes, we're in a state."
                  "No problem, Madam Fran."
"But what if we're not ready when you have to leave, dear man?"
"We'll wait a little longer, just. Now, where d'you want that pan
And kettle? So. You see, it's really just a lot of fun!
And Edinburgh's not so far away, when all is said and done."

Interior Decoration

We had a dark-blue kitchen wall at one time.
"Not **dark blue**! Ultramarine!" she said.
"It won't do," said our decorator, looking sad and shaking his head.
"It will," she said.
"It won't be in the catalogues or shade-cards."
"Mix it," she said.
And he did, in gloss, and it looked GREAT!

"I want an orange bedroom." She was six,
With all her mother's stubbornness.
"No way," we said, "You'll never get to sleep, and nor will Teddy."
"Yes, we will!" And did.
But the trouble we had finding first a paint
That would come off, or we could cover,
Paint from which her crayoned pictures could be sponged,
Without refusing Bluetac.

"I always wanted a garden shed", I said,
    "in pink."
"You're daft!" she said,
"That won't be an opinion unique to me, either.
No-one else will go there."
But they did. A real man-cave it became,
Or at least men. And daughter.
She just can't think why.
("The cellar helps", I said, but she still didn't understand.)

And so the answer, friends, in colour
As in life - "Be Bold, Be Strong,"
Above all else, "Be True to YOU!"
    Just Do It! Sing *your* song!

The Cottage By The Golf Course

On paper, the details were perfect,
Three bedrooms, a bathroom and loo
Upstairs, and downstairs a kitchen,
A dining room, sitting-room too,

With beautiful double-glazed windows,
An aspect of green grass and trees,
With bright flags on sticks in some places,
And squirrels, and sweet birds, and bees.

So I bought it, and Spring was a picture,
And gradually Summer came round,
And the players came out with their golf-balls,
And guess the next thing that I found?

"We-Take-All-Your-Worries-Insurance.
What address? Oh, madam, I fear
Your home isn't covered for windows,
That's been the arrangement for years."

Sealers

Grubby little black ships, greasy-prowed, and chipped
Where carcasses are winched aboard from fouled and bloodied ice,
And lookouts stand in wind and snow, to spot and shoot and clout
The ice-bear and the seals they came to find:
Butting into choppy seas and brash around Bear Island
And the coasts of Svarlbard, where the grinding ice permits,
And glacier-melt marks summer's coming, strengthening tidal streams
To wash the glaciers' calvings to the sea.

Loaded to their licence-level, off they head again
For home in the Lofotens and beyond, where skins
Will represent the booty of their voyage, and make coats
And hats and gloves and trousers for the rich,
And for the workers of the cold-seas' ships.

Just as, so many centuries before, their fathers' ships,
Black-hulled and raven-sailed, came west and south
For booty from the towns and monast'ries of warmer Europe,
Wool-cloth, tapestries and candles, jewels and hand-worked gold,
And went home, grubby with the blood of those
Who dared oppose the Viking men.

Now they are mostly traders, but still some
Feel in their blood the saga-singing voice
Of huntsmen, and respond with courage to the call,
To travel North for pelts and furs, just as their fathers did.

Sonnet To An Old-Fashioned Librarian

I glimpsed you through the nine-one-oh's,
I watched you through the gaps
Between the "Cookery (Europe)"
And the "Paper: Folds and Flaps".
I chose a place and sat there.
Your desk was in full view,
And, though the book I'd chosen bored,
The hours I sat there flew.
But never did your eyelids rise,
Nor your lips part, to murmur
The words of love and comfort which
I longed for in my fervour.
Your library is a silent place, God wot,
But not a place for love to scheme or plot.

At The Marriage Of ...

"Can you see her? Can you see her?"
"'Course I can't, from stuck back here!"
"It'll improve when we all sit down."
"It won't, with Chelsea Flower Show there!"
"It's very artistic. All those flowers
From country gardens, I've no doubt,
And that huge brim and crown, like bowers
And terraced beds below a manor house."
"I'll ask her when I want a twitching hide
For the Birdwatchers' Club. All of them
Could hide behind her, none to be seen again,
      EVER. They'd all be lost.
Oh, now she's leaning sideways. Left. Now right."
"Jack, put away your i-phone. Just relax.
You'll have to see her when they all come back."

Beached People

Here on a bare beach, puffing
Like a landed fish, by my own efforts,
My son in my arms, my daughter with my wife
Offshore. Drowned? And her mother?
Would they all have lived, among the shells
And rockets and explosions in our town
If we had stayed there, rather than migrated
When our world turned black?
Was it my fault, or my decision
Alone? My cousin and my imam had both gone.
The market and the mosque were both just walls
Unroofed, unfenestrated – Yes, I know that word,
For I was educated, architect, a man
Well-known as a professional in our town.
What work will I find now, if any, here?
It will be some time before
I can find food, or clothes, or shelter from the sun,
And then the snow of winter.
And my son? How will he grow, and with what
Principles to guide him? Vengeance, life
Of crime, of preservation, or to beg
Among the litter and the feet
Of passers-by?

Death happened where we lived, but seldom more
Or less than it had ever done. But here,
Dumped from that boat a mile offshore, to swim –
We, from the desert, we had never seen
The sea until the trucks had crossed the sands for days,
We, hungry and dry of mouth, and oh so bruised
From the truck's bouncing on the west-bound track
Marked only by the tyres of those before.

And we had paid for this! A chance to earn
Enough on England's golden pavements, we,
Sent on this deathly journey by old men
Who said it was our duty, so that we
Could send wealth home.

We swam, those of us who could learn to swim
In no time, instinct teaching us at once
How to preserve our lives. Will we be welcome?
Whether so or not, we cannot go back now.
All we can do is struggle on in hope
Of mercy, charity, food and drink, and care.
Why should they welcome us?
Because we're men
Like them, with families like theirs. And strong,
And willing to do anything they ask.
And desperate, as we lie here, and we gasp.

Fireworks

BANG! bang, bang, BANG! Whoosh, kerflub, kerflub, kerflub. "Aaaaarrh!"
Whoosh. Whooosh. Kerflub. BANG! Thrub, thrub, thrub, thrub, kerflub.
Tense pause.
BANG! Bang, bang. Whooooosh. Bang. "Aaaaarrrh". Flub, flub.
"Look at that one!" "Oh, sparklers. I LOVE sparklers".
"No! Don't be silly, Douglas, with all these kids about!"
BANG! BANG, bang, bang, bang.
Pause – fingers over ears.
Whoosh, kerflub.
Flaaaawwww, whoosh, flaaaaawww, whoosh, flaaaawwww, whoosh.
Thrub, thrub, thrub, thrub, thrub. "But who *was* Catherine?"
"Who's for a sausage?" "Ooooh, Mum, no,
Not yet, look, there's a whole lot more to come."
Whooosh, ...keeerBang!....BANG! BANG! Bang!
"That's it folks, except for those next door."

That Hand At Table

The fingers that I touched were long, and slim, and cool, and white,
Worked on the pages of your books, the strings and keys of instruments
You pluck and stroke, encourage, polish, strike.
I brushed them, reaching for a fork as you a glove beside a plate,
As white as linen, white as skin, as death, death of my touch
In brevity, a passage flashing power as from a jewelled hand.
That hand you watched, you touched, you brushed,
Was not your hand to watch, or touch, or brush;
And yet it was one left, momentarily,
As a fly, left lightly, lifted and replaced,
Above the soft prey swimming silently,
And up you rose,
From murmuring depth of conversation left, then right, then left.
Oh, yes, I noticed how your warm, kind eye
Hovered sufficiently elsewhere,
But returned always, always, duteous,
To the care of one more than another.
And now here we are, so many years beyond,
Fingers still reaching out as on that summer night,
Not to be noticed except by you and me.

A Childhood Garden In Kent

I'm told – I can't remember - as a child,
I'd lie contented in my p'ram' to watch
The white cloud float past green leaves in the breeze,
The blossom up above elude my catch.

And then, another day, kicking just gently,
My blanket pushed aside, above I'd see
Handfuls of globules, green still where the blossom
Had been blowing, dancing, for my glee.

Next, dark blood red, the Kentish cherries came,
Ripened at last, tree covered to the top;
And, from my p'ram', cooing encouragement,
I'd watch the neighbours gather in the crop.

But that was then; and even after that,
The Kentish orchards were thrust further back
By houses, roads and shops. Brick armies marched,
Completing England's orchard Garden's sack.

Just recently, however, I was back
Where I was born, and, as so many do,
Looked for my parents' house, and there it was,
Same lawn and tree, but one of, oh, so few.

Into Care

I shall not ever see these things again.
For fifty years, they have been mine, acknowledged
By the greetings of old friends and young,
And former young with youngsters of their own.
    I have grown old here, comforted
In growing pain and lessening action
By confidence of knowing where to find
The satisfaction of my every need. And still
My every need is met, indeed foreseen,
Within these rooms, these floors, these windows' views.

I will be exercised, so that
The fingers I need never raise again
Will neither twitch nor wither, nor my toes
Be any longer reached into a void
      Exploratorily.
I will be served, and then I will be fed.
Thank God, I will be vested,
    But never here, never again here,
      For here is pastland, here is memory.
        Here I have relinquished.
          Here I shall no longer ever go.

Aleppo, 2016

    I should not have come back!
        I should not have come back!
It was hard enough to escape,
        Hard enough to carry my mother,
Or my daughter to carry her baby and lead her younger brother,
Blinded, and bandaged across the eyes
Destroyed by the bomb only three days before,
And my wife and I carrying what food and what water
We could carry in both hands and tie around our backs
Over and round the rubble that had been our house,
   And our neighbours',
And see no-one – we hoped – in the darkness,
And cowering when a gun fired or a shell burst
And the flash lit us up as targets for the snipers who,
Blessed be God, were not very good at their job.

   I should not have come back, but
        After the hospital bombing,
    And I and my son and a doctor were the only remaining people
   To crawl out from the rubble where my son was being treated,
   And the streets were no longer defined by walls but by craters,
   And the only thing that might have been left was the shop,…

So, maybe I shouldn't have tried to come back,
For I'd seen how the house and the shop had been shattered,
But only in darkness. I hadn't seen everything
   Razed to the ground, pulled apart and now pillaged
   As I see it this minute, or think that I see it.

I suppose this was ours…was it?
Doors to the right and the left of our shop were the same
As ours, built at the same time, centuries past,

And my fathers and fathers and fathers had all sold
Their spices and carpets and silks and their cottons
From here in the souk, here, under the curved roof
Above which my women and theirs had their chambers
And looked down discreetly through fret-panelled shutters
To see whether husbands for daughters were coming
To visit their parents in neighbouring shops.

There is danger in coming back here.
Now I see it. Even though there seems no-one,
Who knows if a helmeted head is observing me,
      Lining my chest in the hairs of his sight,
      For no reason except I am here.

   "This is mine! This is mine!" I will shout,
   If he shoots, as I die.
        Why should I all alone remain alive?

II

CHARACTERS KNOWN & UNKNOWN

The Old Toby-Jug Maker

What I remember most are those strong grey thumbs,
And the powdered clay that gathered round his eyes,
And his knees going up and down under his apron,
Driving his flashing wheel round and round and round.

"Oh, they are just jars, and the odd jug", he grumbled,
"If I have some spare clay for a handle, and feel like bending it.
Over here, now, are my hobby," and he turned,
Took a fistful of clay from the marsh of his bucket,
And slapped it down on the steel plate on his bench.
Pulling and stretching and squeezing and rolling,
And adding a coating of slip from his fingers,
And coiling one segment on one, and then another,
To raise the sides straight as a board.

        And then

SLAP goes a hump of wet clay, "That's his nose",
And SLAP goes another, above it, "His eyebrows",
And below, "For the mouth and the chin",
And, aside them, "For ears", a SLAP and another, and then
Those great thumbs start their stroking and shaping and pressing
And moulding and forming, and poking for nostrils and ear-channels.
Eyes are made rounder, eyebrows exaggerated, teeth bared by drawn lips,
And chipped and extracted, scowling or grinning,
And nose pointed upwards or downwards, or rounded, off-centre or straight.

And all of a sudden, as if jumping out of the grey clay,
As if born anew from the womb of his mother again,
"Yes! It's him! It's whats'isname, from the telly! That politician chap!
Good gracious! However did you do that?"
And he turns, just his head, as he reaches for clay for a handle,
And slip for adhesive, and a glance at his glaze-pots,
And grins, oh so wicked.
"Want one of you for the wife?" he says.

Rembrandt – Self-Portraits

Here I am. Youthful. Even a confident smile,
At the beginning of my long career.
Brows raised to question with a great respect
The doubts of clients who my work don't know.
A fresh complexion, creamy. Not too big a nose,
(If I can reduce the shadow), and bright eyes
A-crinkle, friendly, beneath hair constrained
Only a little, 'neath a soft, dark cap
Smeared red and white by bristles waved aloft,
Careless, deep in thought of where the next line,
Next shade, next implied aspect of myself,
Will fall. "Who am I? Who now? Who become?"

Now here, against this wall, among these frames
And canvases unfinished – me again.
(This is not arrogance, but self-concern
To check my eye and hands' development
Against the pressures of the passing times.)
By now, you see, the smile has disappeared.
No longer cocky. Here's a man who knows
A painting can go wrong. Mature, grown up,
Still confident, assured now of a life
Respected for my skill. The head held high
Against a fashionable wall. And cheeks
A little pinker now (for wine does that),
And nose, too. Tiny lines (a fine brush
Needed here) around the eyes. And velvet,
Rich, red velvet for the hat.

And lastly,
Here's me now, a fatter man, eyes sunken
Into flesh gone pale and ashen, peeking
At the world. The same red hat, older now,
Ill-kempt, as is the grey hair which it holds,
Or fails to hold, in place. And yet the skill,
The shaping, contours, colour-choice,
Is still there, is it not?

          I do believe
That I may pass from life, and that quite soon,
But that my paintings will live after me.

Councillor Carter

"Don't you sit there, son!" he warned me,
From within his bush of a beard.
"Don't you sit there. He'll be in right soon,
And he's someone who is to be feared."

So we found another table and chairs,
And, indeed, in a minute or two,
In came a magnificent creature,
As if he was called by his cue.

The pint glass was there already,
Fresh pulled, for him to lift,
And he blew the head off sideways
And drank it all off right swift.

The second pint was ready.
He lifted it and looked round.
He nodded, and everyone nodded back,
And shuffled to give him some ground,

And he took the seat at the table
We'd considered when we had arrived,
Put his pint on the table before him,
And his pipe and his baccy beside.

His trousers were tied at the ankle with string,
And his boots were heavy with mud.
A piece of string encircled his gut,
Or he'd lose it out front in a flood.

Both trousers and waistcoat had seen better days.
They were worn, but would do a bit more
'Cos moleskin would go on for year after year.
They would see out their wearer for sure.

"Who is he?" I asked my informant.
"He's the carter," he whispered back.
"His horses have gone now for many a year,
But he still keeps their brushes and tack.

"And he still takes deliveries all over,
Both before and after his lunch"
(With a wink). "But his evenings are different.
Can you guess what he does? Try a hunch."

I couldn't. "Go on," I invited.
"He's the mayor. And no, I'm not mad.
In a suit and a chain and his dignity,
He's the best one this town's ever had!"

"He got us mains gas and mains sewage,
Which we'd waited for, year after year,
And also, he had all our potholes filled in.
I tell you, he should be a peer!"

And I saw him the following weekend,
Adorned in his suit and his chain,
As he opened the latest farm butcher's,
And was cheered to the skies in the rain.

He is a real man of the country.
Whose heart has a dutiful beat.
So never forget the respect that he's owed
When carelessly choosing a seat.

Working From Home

"Come up here and help me", she commands from the second floor landing.
"I'm working", I shout back. "You're not. You're just thinking, as usual.
You can think just as well up here with me." So I go. "What's the job?"
"It's a bed change." "Who's coming?" "George and Freda", she says,
"I did tell you" "Did you?" Distinctly," she says. "Grab that sheet.
No, not that one, the one without lace for the bottom. And not that way.
It goes right-way-up. And this is the head, with the broad hem."
It matters? I think, but daren't say it. "And mind on that corner.
The wood frame will hurt if…" Too late. Another bruised knee,
And I hop for a minute, and curse like a trooper, but "That won't help,"
She helpfully says.

Back downstairs, "I've a meeting at two," she says. "Can you get your own lunch?
There's cold cuts and pie in the 'fridge. And veggies to peel for this evening."
"Yes, yes," I say, "anything. Leave me. I really have work I must do."
But I don't, of course, really have anything 'special to do. I'll just sit here,
Once she's gone in her finery, in front of my laptop, and I'll think.

Moving House

Oh, we're experts in our jobs. No two years are the same.
We're past the stage of whines and sobs, or pointless, empty blame.

    We knew this when we signed up, accepted it of course.
    It shows in all our plates and cups, each from a different source.

We've lived in English houses, and tropic bungalows.
We've chased out snakes and marmosets, tracked errant overflows.

    We've also lived in Europe, where we ate the local food,
    The soups and cheese and sauces, and the wines
               which changed our mood,

Each country and its menus required a different set
Of cutlery and crockery, quite a lot we'd never met.

    But now we're packing up again. Amazing what you find!
    Much that has driven us insane, some memories too kind.

What Does She Do?

What does she do in an evening?
Once in her well-known hall,
Breathe deeply with relief to be alone, without people, at long last?
Hang up her coat neatly on its hanger,
The one from which she lifted it as neatly that morning?
    Each morning?
Make a weak tea, feed the cat,
And prick and ping a solo supper?
Select her book, settle in her habitual armchair,
Cuddled by cushions from her favourite charity shop,
    And wait for her ten o'clock bedtime
    And the blessed unconsciousness of eight hours sleep?

Or does she throw off her drab brown coat,
Put aside her glasses,
Undress to skin and bathe with oils and candles,
Select red lingerie, sheer stockings, a spangled top,
A skirt shorter and brighter than any seen by colleagues
    Day after day after day?
Is her evening face decorated artistically
With blusher, liner, lipstick, mascara and shadow
That morning faces never, ever see?
Are her heels and head raised a full four inches
Above the levels of the black, flat pumps,
Seen at her morning 'bus stop by her fellow passengers,
Unaddressed, unnoticed, on her way to work?

Does she meet friends in evenings,
Laugh, chatter, drink her share
Of the shared bottles of good wine they take their turns
To buy and pour into big glasses?
Does she dance, when a handsome man
Is bold enough to ask her? Does she take one home,
Occasionally, if he proves especially special?

Or, having made a cup of tea,
Does she lift the laptop's shiny lid
And seek the dating agencies for men -
Or women? – who might fill an hour,
An evening, even perhaps a life,
There, on her lonely sofa,
Among her lonely dreams?

Who is she? How many of us know
Those whom we see each day?
Why should we? Aren't their lives their own?

My Grandpa's Beard

My Grandpa's beard is bushy now,
But once it wasn't so.
My Mummy says that, long ago,
It was all thin and black, just like a crow
Perching on the end of his chin.
I think she didn't like it, but she cried, she said,
When he had to shave it off to get another job
Where they didn't like it either – only more.
Then he looked neat and tidy, I suppose,
And boring, just like everybody's Dad.
Not like my Grandpa in the very least!
Now he's got another one, only white,
With curls under his chin where nobody sees but me
When I sit on his knee and twist my fingers in it
And sometimes pull!

I asked my Grandpa,
"Where did your beard come from?
Marks and Spencer's, or a special beard shop,
Or on-line?" But he said, no, it just grew.
    "Like in the garden?" I asked.
    "Do you have to get dirty,
      And smelly, to make it grow?"
But I don't think so, 'cos my Grandpa
    Always smells nice.

Buttons

My Grandma had a button box,
      Or even two or three.
In each of them the buttons ranged
      From vast to odd to wee.

She only ever sorted them
      On finding gaps or spaces
Where pressing needs for decency
      Were written on our faces.

"Oh, what on earth have you done now?"
      She'd say, as if to flounce,
And reach out for a button box,
      And lose her way at once.

"Now that one's off a jacket
      I had forty years ago.
This yellow one, that's from a dress
      I made for your Aunt Jo.

"It won't do for your trousers,
      But was such a handsome colour!
Now what about this pearly one?
      Too small, that little feller!

"I had this one from Aunty Win,
      Who lived near us in Flore.
We had a pretty little house,
      Real 'roses round the door'"

"Well, that was nice", she'd say, and sigh,
      Expression blank, eyes misting,
Counting her buttons through memories,
      And watching her life's scenes shifting.

Welsh Row, Beam Street

Over the holystoned step, bright whitened every day,
I'd go, school cap pulled on, and tweed coat belted close,
Turn right onto the pavement, and then *run*,
Run like the wind past Marjie's narrow front,
Glancing to see if possibly her face
Might show behind her nets, and, if it did,
Grin, 'cos, underneath her appled-face,
There *was* a sense of humour, sharp and dry.
Then, curving right again, descend the hill
At full speed, past the *special house* below,
White-painted, with a wide-paved carriage space,
Behind a little wall where, homeward bound,
I'd sit to rest legs tired by climbing home.
But, in a morning, even faster still,
With the hill steepening to the Weaver Bridge
(No point in stopping at the tiny shop
Whose wee, dark, toy-filled window demonstrates
The lack of cash 'till Pocket Money Day).
On, on, puff, puff, across the ancient bridge,
So that the Mill Weir's roar, down to the right,
Does not attract me, draw me to its sound,
Into the water to destruction dire.
And now up, twisting left into The Square,
With Smith's the Papers, and the Church on guard.
One corner more, and there's the school gate, open.
Safely here at last!

Views Across The Tyne

Partial poverty. Low, narrow streets. Drab back-to-backs.
Steel river without steel, except for scrap.

Here he played cribbage with car number-plates
In search of work,
    Finding it only in war,
        And through it
            Losing the power of speech.

Returned escapee to the silver river.
Next generation.
    Metro, The Baltic, clubs,
    Bright-painted sills and steps.
    New spirit. Talk.
    Talk everywhere.

Life he would have seen
In silence.
Slow smile,
    Happy for his towns,
    Proud for his people
Whom he did not, will not ever, see.

The Bear's Spring

Big and black and shaggy – that's the car.
Muddy, holed and drab his anorak
As he climbs down outside the general store.
"H'war, Dougal," one or two men bravely mutter.
"Aye," the mass of hair and kilt and boots responds.
Quietly. No-one moves.

"His first words to anither human being
Since the first snowfall last November, now.
It aye taks him a while to warm to people."

"Where's he live?"

"Och, a wee cabin, far, far up yon lane
Beyond the shoppie. Miles up, where it's safe,
He says, from thieves and frauds and scams,
And sheep and deer and birds are alway kindness."

"How's he eat, all winter?"

"Freezers, stocked in Autumn, from here-by,
Stocked to the gun'lls, everything he needs,
And colded by th'electric generator
He had built by his bothy for his heat.

"He's safe enough, and quiet enough, up there,
And Christmas Day we call his telephone
From the shop here, to see he's still alive
And di'sna' want the Dominie and the Kirk
Just yet.

"And Spring, he comes out, like a grizzly bear."
"But tamer."
    "Just."
        "Maybe."

Heritage

This is not where they sat, my forebears,
Squatting, feet flat, legs folded
Like frogs in the corner of a garden,
Backs straight on the hard rock wall,
Near-naked, but not like the summer bodies on Cullercoats beach.
Here, clothed in coal, dark grey like undertakers,
Which they sometimes were when roofs came down.
The only lights for them were pencil-shafts
Shot by their helmet-mounted lamps.

Now, as we troop, with children, in their tracks
Through two-foot galleries opened into caves
Like dance-halls, ceilings far too high to see,
And lit like High Streets,
We can walk upright where they could only crawl;
    And yet, the feeling's awesome!

We come here being curious, they from pride.
"We won the coal", our Grandpa gasps
Through throat and lungs coated with dust, and dying.

And, if he feels that pride, then so must we.

Autumn

"I've oiled and put away the bat long since", he said to me.
"My pads and gloves I've whitened, and stored them in the shed,
And boiled my shirts and flannels, pressed them carefully as well,
Before I laid them in their folds. When I've gone, they might sell."
"I've done my time in long white coats, six pebbles in one pocket,
A panama upon my head, for shade, to see the wicket.
I've even been a scorer, and shared pencils and a joke
In that wee box far yonder, with lots of friendly folk."
"I've chaired the club for many a year, and right good times we've had,
So, when I've gone, I really hope that no-one will be sad."
I've got my season ticket. I'll turn up for every game,
And buy my tea, and greet the lads, but it won't be the same.
It's all these bright pyjama-suits. I never did approve,
But my lot's dusk is falling, and a new day's on the move."

Weekend Neighbours

We sit along the water's edge,
Tucked down into the leafy sedge,
So neither friend nor fish might see
The distance between him and me.

    We never share our bag or bait.
    It's not from coldness or from hate.
    Its just we come, whene'er we can,
    To leave behind our fellow-man.

A flask for warmth, a pasty too,
Our maggots, and our bread rubbed through,
Our lead weights, pliers and nylon thread,
There's hours to pass 'fore time for bed.

    With line and rod and float and hook
    (We're not the lads who'd take a book)
    We concentrate – in fact, we doze.
    It wouldn't matter if we froze.

You see, the world's demands all week
Are quite enough, and so we seek,
At weekends, somewhere quiet to go,
To stand aside beyond, beside, the flow.

The Expert

My Dad could read a football match – he said!
He knew – and loudly offered his advice
To all and sundry round him – when the ball
Was passed inside instead of out, or back
When "Forward, forward, idiot,"
Was all that the play called for.
Every week, he'd sit - though not for long, once the play warmed up –
Attired in warmest coat and team-scarf,
Pie and tea to hand after half-time,
And sing the songs, and chant the chants
His Dad had taught him.
Funny thing (for a dustman), his knowledge also showed
In comments on the referee's eyesight (much deficient)
And the linesmen's fitness ("Couldn't keep up with a goat!"),
Let alone the quality of the groundsman's turf.

And then he lost his voice. Permanently lost it,
Poor chap, and the life went out of him,
For he couldn't bring himself to go to matches
Where he couldn't help the team on with his advice.
Thank goodness for TV, my Mother said, as she went out
For Saturday shopping when the match came on.

No "Click-And-Drop" For Me!

Wheee! It's ME! Standing in the prow,
Cutting through the shoppers like a man with a plough.
Wheee! It's ME! Helping Mum to shop.
Lifting stuff she's never seen, shopping fit to drop.

My older sister Emeline insists she's very modern,
And shops at midnight, on returning from the local tavern.
But Mum declines the joys and thrills of all this techno-lodgy
When all she wants to buy is beef, and p'raps a nice fresh caulie.

"I like to see and feel" ("and taste", say I) "what I might buy.
I've got to take it home and keep it, so it can't be dry."
But I don't worry what we get, as long as I can reach it,
And Dad eats anything, it seems. Here comes a tin of peaches!

I wave and shout to all my friends here, shopping with their Mums.
We're pirates, Vikings, South Sea men, exploring unknown oceans.
It doesn't matter what we are, we say. At least we're sure
That "Let's pretend" is better fun than sit at home some more.

Now, steady on, the manager's approaching down the aisle.
It's time to sit low, quietly, until he passes by;
And, at the check-out, I must help my poor Mum to remember
   What she habitually forgets,
      Her blessed plastic-number.

Love Is Not Everything

Love is not everything,
But leave me not quite bereft
Of everything,
Touch, smell, sweet taste, occasional sight.
Am I to wither unloved? May at least
The heart of a dear friend not be petrified,
Turned to hard, weathered stone,
Be runnelled down by tears
Too out-of-age for any dignity?
I need to love you, and I need at least
Affection, friendship, for my dying years,
'Else I shall dry, withdraw into myself
Alone, and be a pitiable thing.
Smile on me, dearest, just from time to time.

Next Door

My nearest neighbour, Mrs. Rowse,
Just down the lane, quiet as a mouse.
Of her I never hear a sound,
Or know for sure if she's around.

   Now, Mrs. Benn, and her boy Bryn,
   Who live the other way, a pin
   Would have to weigh a ton, it's clear,
   To make an impact on the ear.

"Bryn's going to be a Ringo Star,"
She'll tell the world in any bar,
"And practice!" "Yes, we know, my love,
The dead can hear it from above."

   But, when the river floods, guess who
   Will mash the tea and let it brew
   While bread is cut and cake dished out
   For everyone from round about?

"A treasure, Mrs Rowse," they say,
"Kindness itself in every way,"
While Bryn and Ma, with drums and sticks,
Still shout for rescue from their fix.

Caravaggio

Dark, dark, the windows shuttered,
But for one shaft of light,
Or candles close beneath a tortured face.
Anger, always anger, that he should be driven here
To paint with anger, cutting with his brush
As with a dagger, cutting into life,
Until his tongue and blade, in a dark alley,
Cut too deep.

      Then, flight, fleeing the magistrate
South out of papal lands to start again,
But still in paint, his ever only skill,
Still dark, and hard, and angry
'Till the day they found him and he fled again,
Back to the North, protesting innocence,
And, fearful of his great persuasive power,
Fearful he would escape, they used his paint
To poison him, to cause a unique life,
Tortured by pain, to end.

Spring In A Winter Place

Warmth, in the day if not at night,
Through a small corner pierced in frosted-glass.
Via a brief gap, the chestnut leaves at last
Begin chlorophyll-filled unfurling, whispering up
Into a blue-white sky.
Boredom and noise, always boredom and noise.
Banging of doors, and feet on stairs, and cups on handrails,
And threats all round, despite the bars and locks.
Not our locks, not *my* locks, designed to keep *me* safe.

Winter, always winter here inside,
Whatever might be seen briefly outside
On marches to and from and round and round.
No sign of sea or cliff or gull or sun,
Though I can smell and feel and hear them all.
They are not mine.
And yet the chestnut branch
Is mine, by right of sight!
Until the glass is mended,
I can watch leaf and blossom in their turn.
Will I still be here in conker-time?

I should not be here!
Everyone says it, but for me it's true. I didn't do it,
Or, at least, not as they say I did.
It wasn't my hand, not my boot, my car....
And I will never, *ever* let my mind
Trap me again into needing friends like them...

Or will I, when the Spring and Summer pass,
And, on my own, without a job,
With Winter coming on, without a home,
Will I come back here? Is there some way through
To an alternative path? Can my life branch away
From what is normal here, a way of life
      Without the noise and threats?

Even in Spring, this is a Winter place.

Valentine For A Long-Standing Relationship

I saw you at the Village Hall
So full of youth and vigour,
But you have cooked so long for me
You've shrivelled up my liver.

   The sight of you excited me,
   It left me all a-quiver.
   Now when you come too near to me
   It always makes me shiver.

We strolled the length of Lovers' Lane,
We cuddled by the river.
Now when you reach your hand to me
I fear what you'll deliver.

   But even so, here we remain,
   Apparently light-hearted.
   They think we are so much in love.
   We never will be parted.

Khrushchev's Shoe

(On 11 October 1960, Mr. Khrushchev, President of the USSR, took off a shoe and hammered it on a table at a UN General Assembly, when his country was accused of East European colonialism)

Nikita Khrushchev was angry!
Nikita Khrushchev was cross!
The damned Philipino had talked long enough.
No-one said that Nikita was posh!

Nikita cared nothing for manners.
His feet hurt, and nothing was said
That he understood without headphones,
And they scratched at the top of his head.

And his feet hurt. His dear wife had bodged up
A hole in the top of his sock,
But the sweat and the bored-stiff discomfort
Were making his whole body rock.

At last, in sheer absolute trauma,
Nikita reached down to his heel,
And ripped off his shoe – but continued
The dreadful discomfort to feel.

So he hammered the shoe on the table.
The hon'rable speaker just stopped.
The American President's guardsmen
Shot hands to their guns, but then mopped

Sweating foreheads, on seeing Nikita,
Not a gun but a shoe in his hand,
And everyone laughed quite politely
With relief, as peace spread through the land.

The Engineer And The Poet

"I'm only a horny-handed, dirty-nailed engineer," you said,
But I saw the precision with which those hands
Selected pen, and tool, and knife and fork at table.

Once, you worked your perfection to produce
Surfaces that shone like the face of the sun,
Screamed as they whirled, flashed like the source of all light,
Louder and brighter than eye or ear could bear;
And I saw in your pocket the weight of your polished micrometer.
Nowadays, photo-electric microscopes measure to units of microns.
Once, hand and eye lined the jaws, spun the gauge, to a few thou',
And you were proud, and held in high regard
For the levels of accuracy that your skill achieved.

"Only" was never a word for an engineer:
   Nor for a poet.
Words can be slopped about by those who are careless,
But poets dispose of their words with pedantic precision,
Selecting, then whittling, then honing, and trying for size,
Then whittling again, maybe throwing away a whole line
Before choosing exactly the word their intention requires.
Poets are engineers of meaning and message.

Deride neither poets nor engineers, deaf though they are
To the rest of the "that'll do" world they've both left behind.

What Do You Make?

Well, I'm a teacher. I make lives, you see,
Identifying talent, and encouraging those who can and will,
Maybe no more than one a year, but, oh,
When they succeed, the feeling of fulfilment swells my heart.

Me? I'm a cabinet-maker, making drawers that slide
Like silk, silently. In and out they glide,
Expose and hide everything dear to whomsoever may
Buy my transformed bare wood and skill.
The work and polish of one life, offered
For generations coming after me.

I make the roads you drive on. Once, a gang
Was needed to strip off the surface tar,
And heat and spread replacement surfaces
So that they are safe. Now, one machine, one man,
Can do that work, with just another two
To dig out manhole covers, drains and such.
We keep the country going, you might say.

A butcher, me, just like my Dad was too,
Who taught me as his Dad had tutored him.
This was my Grandpa's knife and steel. D'you see
How worn the ivory in this handle's gone?
But still the best I've found.

Yes, 'course we had a shop! All of us, handed down.
Not now, of course. With rent and rates and pay,
I s'pose I should be grateful I'm employed
Here in this supermarket, doing what I know.
But, yes, I miss not having one my own.

A programmer, me. I learnt some skill at school,
Cracking security on the school website, first,
Then that on the Head Teacher's system.
Now I make a living writing security programmes
For banks, for company Human Resources groups,
For anybody, really, who will pay.

I was a steel-worker, when I was in work.
I poured the steel into the moulds. Hot work it was,
And heavy, but a man could take a pride
In working there. I've been out on the road
Since all that ended, forty years ago. Couldn't do
With office-work, not what suited me,
Or the back-biting where the most that's asked
Is press a key, repeat a message given on a screen.
So I make nothing but this bothy here,
For when it's cold, and others down the roads,
And traps for varmints, when I need to eat.

I am a politician. We make and we break lives,
Mostly for good, for those who have the drive
To deserve prosperity, sometimes to right a wrong,
Though often all we're doing is to change
The balance in society which upheld
One group against another. Yes, it's true
Sometimes our Acts and Regulations wipe away
Whole industries, communities, traditions,
But that is progress, and we must go on
To a bright future. Can't be left behind!

Martyred By Lions

So many broken heads and hearts,
    So many broken dreams,
Shattered by uncaring
For the skills and structures and knowledge
    On which we dreamt as children,
    Worked in youth,
    Believed and crafted
As maturity crept up and passed,
And we gave up our lives
That they might love as we had loved.

Such deep exhaustion. Like a garden cane,
We have been driven deep into the encompassing mud
By blows repeated and repeated,
    Shouted jeers, frustration!
"It <u>is</u> good and right and useful.
Believe with us!"

But no. So few today will see it,
Be allowed to see it by the pressure of their peers;
    And we are broken by the hundred,
    Deserted by the young and old who,
    Before us, saw that what is devastated
    Is best left behind, or pulls us down.

So now we sit, crew on a sinking ship,
    Hurt, aching,
    Sore in head and heart,
And the bell shrills to drag us yet again,
Broken, before our predators,
    As if in chains.

Victim's Possessions

The last policeman hoists his frozen hands
From the rain-sodden, leaf-strewn tarmac of the road,
Strips off his rubber gloves, snap, snap, and shakes,
So gently, the last plastic bag for the Forensics crew.
All gathered in, now, remnants of a life
Smeared out beneath the truck she never heard,
Crossing the road and texting to her friend
Coincident with him accelerating round the corner
To the beat of a new playlist tune, and looking up
Too late.
The O-'s of mouths and eyes of passers-by,
The screams of children and of ambulances,
All gone now. Just this wee bag of uncapped lipstick,
Specs-case, tissue, emptied purse, and 'phone,
Cold-frozen, sodden, in the tragic rain.

The English Mystery

One thing I'll never understand
Is why the boundary must be manned
By someone portly, without speed,
Who warning shouts can never heed
Because his eyes have never see'd
Th'approaching ball lift off the bat,
Wing on towards him, and...that's that,
A four, a six, beyond his reach.
Can no-one this man ever teach
The mysteries of this game?

I was that man. Compulsorily,
They'd put me where I could not see
The bat or ball or stumps or lines
Of crease or boundary. Every time,
I'd face the sun, my glasses glazed
By sweat from running, quite amazed
That "Over!" would be called so fast.
I could not grasp six balls had passed,
        And I had not seen one!

I must admit, the names they called
Might well be whispered as be bawled.
They made no sense to me.
Mid-on, mid-off (no switches here),
Leg-slip, not foot, a gully mere,
But not a hole or pit to trip.
Square Leg? Well, that one does beat all!
        But worst of all was batting.

"You'll go in last", they always said.
"That's safest." But it seems I'm bred
To never bat – we'd win or draw –
Or else to hear that hoary saw,
"Just stay there, let the others slog.
Defend. Stone-wall. Straight bat. Don't flog
At everything. Four balls is all
There are left." Then I'd hear a call
To run, and know, "I can't get there",
And everyone would frown and glare
        As I walked in ashamed.

I only played 'cos they were short.
My best friends, when asked, gave a snort,
And said they wouldn't waste their time.
But I was always soft. They'd mime
A graceful shot. I'd see me play
Just so upon the coming day.
I loved the smiles and warmth they gave
Until I had forgot their rage
The last time that I joined their team.

Ah well, life turns just as the seam
Of a red leather sphere misleads.
        Why do we do what we foresee
        To lead alone to mystery?

III
CATS & OTHER CREATURES

Sunny

In the midst of the Visitors' Parking, he sits and washes 'till they've stopped
And abandoned their car to his attentions.
Then he seeks out the forensic details of their journeys,
Nose to tyre, nose to hubcap, paws on wheel, and nose all round
Within the black wheel arch, and, with half a chance, the boot.

Not a young cat. Seldom rushes, though he can!
His huge territory needs thorough patrolling first thing, starting with the sun,
Before the squirrels stir in the golf-course trees.
Handsome tail, and broad white whiskers, and a straight, frank look
At everyone he meets, although not all are graced with greeting.
Not all deserve it. He has business, here and o'er the fence,
        and then long gone.

But back a little later, back along the kerbstone by the grass,
Duties done, whatever they may be,
And ready for a cuddle down beside the kitchen door,
Where 'specially understanding people may be trusted
To supply a pusscat's needs of food and drink and shelter,
        And a blanket for his warmth.

The Visiting Dragon

He comes in the night, growling through the dark.
In the hours before dawn, he disturbs us,
While minds are still blank and relaxed in sleep.
Like a huge yellow bat, he pings, tail-first,
Into the drive, creeping between the cars,
Fire flashing from either side of his head,
Eyes beaming like lighthouses, swinging on
Our windows, roaring now with strength and power,
To the place where he feeds on the rubbish
Prepared for him, sacrifice-like, in its bins.
And he stops, and his pilot-fish helpers
Run his bins to his rear-facing mouth.
He stoops, lifts, sucks hard, and shouts out aloud,
As his heartbeat pounds.
Then, his food all consumed, and its bins back
Where they live, he withdraws down the road home,
To hide from the daylight he seems to fear and dread;
And we, wide awake, can only dread too
The coming day, lacking sleep's energy.

Cat, Dreaming

Cat sleeps, curled, nose buried, whiskers bent,
Ears tidy, pointed, tail curved round, paws in,
Until a dream arises from the dark
Of her unconscious mind.
    A little scrabbling sound of tiny feet.
        Where is it? Ears begin to turn
    This way and that, in twitches.
    There it is! Stalking, a leg comes out
        To reach, eyes closed, towards the tiny sound,
    And, from the ankle, leaps.
Now tail uncurls, flaps, thrashes,
And her eyes, still closed, begin to flicker.
    But the dream escapes,
        And cat relaxes,
            Draws in leg and tail,
Turns head just slightly further from the fire,
And settles back to deep, unhaunted sleep.

Sonnet Of New Life

Fatter, fatter, fatter grow the flanks of the shy deer,
Gentle-eyed, thin-legged, unsure how this occurred
Sometime last Autumn-Winter, deeply hid,
By coyly shuffling edges first towards, away,
Towards again, ears forward, ears laid back,
And after all of that now this, laid low
In the newly-sprouting heath-land grass
Between twigged shrubby bushes, glowing green
With the new buds.
          No-one sees the tiny bundle
'Till it stands to reach for mother, suckling
Its first strength-giving milk, wobbling, bobbing
At her teat, on legs unsure and eyes nowhere
Except for she who has given life, will teach
What life is for and how a kid should live.

Steps

If I were not a man, I'd be a gull,
With wide, broad wings to sit upon the wind
And fly above the sea in lapping turns
Observing gentle waves on which to land
And float, tail cocked, to doze in peace and quiet,
Or see a fishing boat hauling its nets
And so providing food for crew and me,
Or, as the wind rose, let it sweep me with it
Inland. What land? Who cares? All are the same
To one not needing language, only space.
But, best of all, to fly home to my place,
Hoisting my wings into the wind to stall
Precisely on the step where I was born
And where my chicks grow up in their own place
On that same towering cliff of steps
Where each, like human beings, knows the height
To which Creation has allotted them,
However they may squabble to ascend.

Prejudices And Realities

Black cats come from London.
   Ginger cats are Toms.
Siamese talk all the time,
   And comb their coloured points.
Tabby cats are stripy,
   And spotty underneath,
Their lovely wavy whiskers
   Reflect the sun in glints.

Farm cats are all shaggy,
   'Cos no-one brushes them.
They come in every colour,
   And creep out of every den.
White cats all have topaz eyes,
   Or silver-blue, of course.
Whichever, every one of them
   Is deaf, and has big paws.

Whatever colour they may be,
   With patience and a treat,
You can tempt every one of them
   To join you on a seat,
And cross their paws, and blink their eyes,
   And say, "Here I belong",
And stay there with you, quite content,
   Purring their loving song.

Bought At The Sales

"I got it at the sales, of course,
      It's nothing that we need.
I liked its colour at first sight.
      It won't cost much to feed."

"I couldn't just ignore it, now,
      That wouldn't have been right.
The other one's a friendly type,
      There'll never be a fight."

"Our Gran will find a bed for it,
      Aunt Jessie's got a blanket.
It eats quite tidily, I'm told
      And it can have my bucket,

"And I can take it up to school
      For everyone to study,
And if I'm careful where it steps
      The classroom won't get muddy."

But even as I practised this,
      I knew it wouldn't do.
Mum wouldn't ever let me keep
      A lion stained white and blue.

Gabble-Gobble

Tom Turkey went to London,
    To join the B.B.C.
He thought that might be difficult,
    But he thought he'd go and see.

They didn't turn him out at once.
    "Oh no," they said, "We're fair.
We'll try you out with others first.
    A turkey here is rare."

An audience they first procured,
    To judge which one was heard
Most clearly through the microphone.
    The contrast was absurd.

"Quack-quack," the test-piece banker said,
    At break-neck stumbling speed,
So Tom replied, "Gob-gobble",
    But the banker took no heed.

"Quack-quack, quack-quack-quack, quack again,"
    The banker then insisted,
And Tommy gobbled quietly
    While the banker turned and twisted.

"Well done, our Tom," producers cried
    From all around the floor,
"You had him in a proper mess!
    You quite showed him the door!"

"You've got a job for life here,
    You can read the business news
Each morning, early, every day."
    Our Tom was quite bemused.

"A-gobble-gobble-gobble",
    Said our Tommy gratefully,
And walked down to the Beeb canteen
    For his first cup of tea.

Owl

Close to the grass-tops,
Silently, silently,
Gliding, his eyed face
Down-turned, so reflecting
The sights and the sounds from below,
From the creatures
His family need for the growth of their fledglings.

Soaring, and soaring,
Still silently, silently,
Seeking the wood's edge,
Where tree-trunks and bushes
Give way to the grassland,
And creatures try vainly
To hide in the rootlings,
But cannot escape him.

Wings hugely flapping,
But silently, silently,
Driving him powerfully
On through the forest,
Drawn in and upward
To speed between branches,
Then laid horizontal
To glide on again.

Nearing his nestlings,
He squeaks through his sharp beak,
Turns up his chest and spreads out his broad tail,
Hands over his catch to his partner, their mother,
And swings round once more as he takes to the air.

"But why won't he hoot?" you may ask, disappointed.
"Oh, he is so much, much too clever for that.
If he did as he hunted they'd all hear him coming.
Just wait till he's killed, then he'll hoot, long and flat,
In a note that will carry all over his country,
To say, 'We will eat', and "I'm on my way back.'"

In Pusscat's Power

She sits and watches from the dresser shelf
Where I have given up my silly fears
For the best saucers. Then she reaches down
Like a coiled spring, controlled, and drops front feet
Then back ones onto all the notes I made
Laboriously, gradually, slow,
With care for each and every word I chose,
And spreads herself across them, tail fluffed out,
Chin in among the furry neck-ruff, like
A scrum-half spread to cover all the ball
From the opposing forwards. Then she grins
- She does! – at me, frustrated, waiting
For her time to let me see what she
Has captured, in addition to my love
And my attention.

      Well, at least, I can
Open the keyboard cover. Once exposed,
She moves, of course, a shuffle, effortless,
Onto the keys, and rubbish hits the screen.
But so it would have done, had I been typing,
And she is prettier far than I compose.

IV
SOUL POEMS

Midnight Sparrow

Darkness in here by seven,
After I've helped the Rector say Evensong
And we've tweeted through the psalms and canticles.

But not tonight.
Just after seven, actually,
And I with my head beneath my wing
On my favourite beam where I could see the Rood if I awoke,
On came the light by the vestry door,
And in came the Sacristan, brocade and linen in hand
To dress the Sanctuary all in white and gold.

By about eight, there was no chance of sleep for me
With the twitter of female human voices
Discussing the angle of every bough and thorn of holly,
And where might we get just a few more candles
   To light up the hymn books in the dark.

By eleven, the choir were assembling,
Boys laying out book after book after book
On the stalls,
While others peered round the vestry door and whispered
'Till hushed sharply by a fierce-looking elderly man
With half-glasses and a white, flappy surplice
On his way to the organ.
   "Oh my, this is going to be big!" I thought to myself.

And it was!

What a mass of people there were to fit in!
Some knew where to sit, some had no more idea than how to fly,
Clearly "once-a-yearers", but 'specially welcome on this special night.
Once sitting, they whispered and greeted each other
With excitement unbounded by the time, or the sight,
To begin with, of clergy and servers and crucifer
Down by the open West door.

Then, gradually, quiet, and I fluffed out my feathers
And settled myself to watch over the service,
And join in the worship of Christ come to Earth
As a baby, as all of us once were.

Finally, sure enough, poor Rector, exhausted,
Walked down to the front of the altar, and said
"Happy Christmas to everyone!"
And everyone cheered him, and, up in the tower,
      Bells rang,
            And it felt as if Jesus laid hands on our heads.

Fatherhood

You must have been terrified, Joseph,
A reluctant husband, new wife already with child,
And then this journey from Galilee,
Winter's cold, and the wind on the hills of Judea
Cutting you both to the quick, and the donkey,
      And no grazing.
And now, no lodgings, and occasional moans already
From the small, frail girl bent over the donkey's neck.
You are not a cold man, but you're practical.
You need a bed for her, urgently.
"Sorry, old man. Full up. Try further down."
Whatever more could you do?

And then, "Well, there's the cave." "Where?"
"Down the back, down that path to the back.
Can you see? It's a stable, so don't light a lamp, or a fire,
For fear of setting light to the straw, and our animals. And yourselves!"

Stumbling, even the donkey, in the dark,
      But there it is.
Dark. How on earth will she manage
If the baby does come?
      "Oh, its coming, its coming,
      Get me down, Joseph,
          please get me down!"
And you did, and it was, and she did,
She and the Old Wife from the inn, who heard her,
And came to bring Him into the world.

And The Cars Went By

He looked from his small bedroom window
As he'd done every morning for years,
But this was the morning of Christmas,
And still the odd car went by.

Nonetheless, today, there'd be strangers
In the pews of his church over there,
And he'd say the service with joy, on this day,
As outside, the cars would go by.

And after the service they'd go home to lunch
With turkey and crackers and wine
And granny and grandpa and children galore
As the cars of late-comers went by.

And, would you believe, by the church-wall,
There was newsprint piled up in a heap
Like a fly-tip, a bonfire, their edges a-stir
As occasional cars would go by.

It was there when he'd finished his luncheon
And returned to his bedroom to pray
As always he did, feast or feria,
While rarely a car still went by.

But then, as he watched, it was moving,
And a figure emerged from the pile.
   He'd been there all day,
   All alone on This Day,
   Burrowed deep in the heap
     For what warmth he could get;

And he gathered his papers
And folded them carefully,
Tucked them away,
And he picked out a pack
From the debris behind him,
Walked off with it
Mounted across his bent back,
   As the evening's first cars went by.

Christmas, Here And Now

If Christ were born on Christmas night today,
Laid in a manger in a barn, and found
By shepherds, they would 'phone for help,
              and soon
Workers from Social Services would come.
He would be homed, or even hospitalised,
His parents jailed, and Magi with their gifts
   Ignored as wandering nutters.

    No, but really,
  What if Christ had been born here?
    Even here and now?
  Could we manage?
      Would we know?
  How would He His Good News sow
     In this modern world?

He would need a Facebook page.
Who would notice, else?
He would need to write a blog,
But, if He did, what of the Trolls
   That hate the serious?
He would need advertisements
On billboards and TV,
A video, appearances on stage and screen,
     With ME!

   No, He would not.

Never for Him was the need for more than a house,
The corner of a garden, the open road, on which to teach
A handful of believers, friends who'd live or die
And, either way, co-operate in offering miracles
Of change or rising live from deathly tomb
As He did on a hidden Sunday morn.

When Christ will next come, maybe Christmas Day
Or Thursday fortnight (not for us to know),
And how (on clouds with angels, or in manger born),
He'll surely be the same as ever, as He's always been.

    The sadness is that so we'll always be.

Coincidences?

Why was that beggar in that place at that time?
Why was that woman held for that especial crime?
Why was their healing and forgiving so sublime
        When Jesus passed?

Why did I meet her in that club those years ago?
Why did that car that missed me drive so slow?
Why did I stoop to find that book, stacked down so low?
        Did Jesus pass?

Was that coincidence? Was God about?
Was that His secret voice giving me a shout?
Perhaps, if I listen, not just shut Him out,
        Jesus will pass!

You Are The Other

You are the Other.
Into You we seek to merge
In prayer, our sins to smother
Through one momentous surge
      Of Love
        From You to us.

You are the Other
Whom we cannot match.
Praying, we might recover
Something, hope that we can snatch
      A taste of love
        From You to us.

You are the Other,
Help that we require
To guide us, as our Father.
Emplace in us Your Fire
      Of Love
        From You to us.

Questions

You asked, "Do you believe in…"
    Jesus, Bible, miracles.
You meant, "What is…"
    God's love, a sacrament.

How can I tell you?
You must search and learn
    And struggle for yourself.

"But where?" you asked.
"Come with me." "Into Church?"
    Your horror palpable in face and limbs.

But afterwards, and next week afterwards,
        and next,
You'll make a start.
        And God will do the rest.

Doubt And Faith

Joseph doubted Her virginity.
It took a dream from God to make him see.

    Nathanael, sceptical of Nazareth,
    Just needed Jesus' vision to confess.

Sinner Matthew/Levi left the tax
To join in Jesus' healing of the lax.

    Little Zacchaeus had to climb a tree,
    And dine with Jesus so that he'd agree.

Thomas needed nail-holes to believe.
Feeling them, "Lord and God: to this I'll cleave!"

All these began from disregarding God.
Belief for them was nothing but a plod.
Jesus said, "Come and see", to all of them.
For each of us He can do just the same.

The Solution Was There All The Time!

*Crystals and diet and numerology,
Potions and creams and reflexology,
Acupuncture, analysis and psychotherapy.
    Nobody's thinking of God.*

Everyone's rushing, they're all under stress,
Marital breakdown and deep loneliness.
What can we do to make us feel better?
    Nobody's thinking of God.

*Crystals and diet and numerology,
Potions and creams and reflexology,
Acupuncture. analysis and psychotherapy.
    Nobody's thinking of God.*

There sits the Church, all quiet and still,
Everyone passes it, there on its hill.
No-one goes in. They've too many worries.
    Nobody's thinking of God.

*Crystals and diet and numerology,
Potions and creams and reflexology,
Acupuncture, analysis and psychotherapy.
    Nobody's thinking of God.*

God has existed since time began.
A wink of His eye is the sum of our span.
And yet we run hither and thither and yon,
    And nobody's thinking of God.

Crystals and diet and numerology,
Potions and creams and reflexology,
Acupuncture and psychoanalysis.
     Nobody's thinking of God.

Where Is It, And What Is It For?

We are not yet machines.
Lots of people in the same shop won't buy
   The same thing (unless it's an i-phone,
And then they'll buy cases in different colours).
Prick us, we will all bleed.
Tickle us, we will all laugh;
But make us an offer, with a cost,
And we'll all choose differently.
That's what the soul is for – one of its purposes, anyway –
To store the values by means of which we choose
Between good and bad, grasp tightly or reject.
But how does little Joe or Jo decide
What characteristics of a thing their soul
Will value, or perhaps straightway ignore?

We learn by trial and error what behaviours
Most benefit us in this life, and so
Our soul learns values from our peers and mentors,
From parents and from neighbours as we go,
As well as from what gives us joy or pain.

The same way does our soul relate to others.
In empathy, we feel what gives them pleasure
And learn experience's lessons that will tell
The Golden Rule – that we were born to do
To others as we hope they'll do to us.

And the soul learns this, stores it, holds it,
Reproduces it when called upon,
Defends it, when temptation's selfish muscle
Stirs the unconscious mind from darkling sleep;
And, by the repetition of its learning,
Prepares us, for there's always more to come.

Wakefulness

Sleep. Sleep. Oh, for the gift of sleep!
Darkness, darkness. Nothing to see through the eyes,
      But through the mind, memories of the heart,
      Memories in daylight long forgotten,
      Blotted out by action, blotted consciously,
But now returned, hovering, haunting, conscience-driven,
Driving back the very front of sleep.

And yet, is sleep a gift? When once asleep
Control of thought is passed from me to dreams
Which rise unsought and uninvited, aching, scaring,
      Comforts beyond hope of happening,
      Scenes beyond experience anywhere.
      Wishes, or fears, or plans, or re-enactments
      Dressed in new clothes, confusing.

By morning, shall we remember them?
On waking, shall we better understand
Whatever meaning our unconscious mind
Has offered up, during the darkling night?
Some, maybe. Will review improve our lot,
And that of those around us? Sometimes, yes.
      Better to sleep untroubled, and gain strength
      For the next day's occasions and demands?
      Well, maybe so – or maybe not, again.

Ah, what a mystery sleep is!
      May it come without delay!
           And may day's night pass always peacefully!

Diver

Diver,
Flip over backwards
Into the pitchblende blackness of my mind
    Down through the inky water
        Seeing what you can find.

I know what I can feel and measure,
Much of what I can call to mind and remember.
This is my consciousness, and does not matter.
    Here I can choose to see or to repress.

Go deeper.
Dive down further to the pearls
Of what I cannot know or cause to rise,
    What has existed everywhere, for ever
        As mystery, as current, or as power.

Symbols of all Creation ever held,
Visioned as gods and goddesses, soul and flesh,
      But undeniably me when they do rise
        Whether I see them, know them, or do not.

Diver,
Return with knowledge. Tell me then
What in particular swirls in my deepest mind
So I may see them coming, and prepare
      To live without the conflict of denial.

Lidded Pots

Submerged beneath molasses, there they float,
Hardly apparent, pale, white, spherical
Pots, with central circled lids, a stump
By which to lift them, if they rise again.
Meanwhile, tight-packed and tamped in hard they lie,
Those thoughts that once I'd think and hope, let die
When aspiration and ambition starved
The soul of them. A whimper, not a cry,
Would mostly see them off, if that. There's some
I put aside without regard at all
When other self-importance pushed them out
Of sight and mind, and even memory.
But one or two remain regrets, and rise
From my unconscious. Waking or asleep.
They shake me, conscience-struck. What did I lose?
What was the balance there? Did I do right?
Can I regain it? No, the lids stick fast
With the firm glue of time and circumstance.

Sunday

Genesis 2, 2-3
On the seventh day, God completed the work He had been doing.
God blessed the seventh day and made it holy, because on that day
He had rested after all His work of creating.

    God gave an example; it's never enough.
    The Israelites still filled their Sabbath with stuff.
    So God made a Law, as a sort of rebuff.
    "You need to take rest on a Sunday."

Exodus 20, 8 and 11
Remember the Sabbath and keep it holy. God has blessed the Sabbath
and made it holy.

    We still need that Law, which Jesus repeated.
    We need to be still, whether standing or seated,
    Or our bodies and spirits will wear out, defeated.
    "You need to take rest on a Sunday."

Matthew 28, 1, 6 and 8
Towards dawn on the first day of the week, Mary of Magdala and the
other Mary went to visit the sepulchre. The angel of the Lord said to them,
'He is not here, for He has risen.' Filled with awe and great joy,
the women ran to tell the disciples.

    Our Lord rose on Sunday. Where else should we go
    Than to church with our brethren, where His blessings flow,
    And be recreated, so that we will all know,
    "We need to be here on a Sunday"?

To A Monastery Guesthouse

Silently, separately, when I first came,
I crept into the warm welcome of this house,
Knowing I did not know why it was here,
What I should do.
>Joyfully, joyfully, I come now, running,
>To rejoin and offer that welcome,
>Knowing it is here for You.

Centuries of nuns and monks have offered this warm welcome,
Rule of Benedict and Will of God,
Provision of soul-food for those in need
At Mass and Hours and meals,
Or in the unseparate silence
Of a private restoration
Of body, mind or soul
As need requires.
Pilgrimage journeys within these walls are made
From desolation to all sorts of joy.
Comfort is found here, gifts of God,
Direct, or through these passing souls
Whose souls touch mine.

Once sipped,
This elixir of health always remains
In memory, to re-emerge as beacon
When the waves rise high
And danger threatens to o'erwhelm us.
>Here we fly, poor broken things,
>For re-creation through their angel-wings.

Merton

Through a birch-wood, in the morning sun
A path meanders on which deer might run
Or rather walk, for in this place is calm
And nothing's heard except a rhythmic psalm.
Even the birds fall quiet for respect,
As if, between their tasks, they might reflect
The glories that their Maker lays out here,
And view His gifts with a small, grateful tear.

You find the path between the bush and fern
Before the abbey door. There you must turn,
Quite fearless, for as yet there is no sign
To indicate you've found the sought-for line.
But cast about. Not too far off your track
You will see pressed-down grasses, and a lack
Of roughness, smoothed by passing feet,
      Not many, maybe.

          Ah, a wooden seat
For those whose energy is failing now
Near journey's end. And, in the flow
Of fresh clear air, a perfume gently floats,
An incense, silent as the prayers it coats.
Grey through the slim trunks seems to peep a wall,
A low door, window, roof, from which will fall,
In a good wind, the thatch which grips its edge,
Trusting in rusted pins to keep their pledge.

"Merton", he greets me, stretching out a hand,
A friendly grin as broad as this broad land
I've crossed to find him. "So they let you come.
So, welcome! Join me." Voice round, like a drum.

No armour here, no snorting steed to ride
To battle with temptation on each side.
I came to learn his strength, a pilgrimage
To make a gain the world can never gauge.

Eight Stones

Orange sand. Evenly grained, flat as a tablecloth,
Iron-rich orange sand. And eight white stones.
No thyme bush, butterfly-adorned, up here.
No tree, no shade, as far as eye can see.
Just eight white stones, laid on the edges of a square
Of orange sand.
And a strong feeling of holiness. "Don't go in!
It is a holy place", he says. "A holy man lived here
Long, long ago, alone with God."
"How did he live? How did he live *here*?", I ask.
"Who fed him? Brought him water?" "Who knows?
Maybe angels fed him. He was bless'd."

And I remembered, on high hills at home,
Green there with grass, not orange sand, a place
Where stones still stand as remnants of a wall,
And lintels mark the door, and window-frames
   Show where the sun lit psalm-books,
    And the holy men honoured their God,

       And it was just the same.

Sunrise, On May-Morning

See that church tower? They used to sing from there
At dawn, each First of May,
Anthems of praise for the glory and power of creation,
And the cows in the fields turned their heads,
    And the horses twitched their ears, and shook their manes,
        And the hens clucked softly, and shifted on last night's eggs.
No longer. The choir's too old and few,
And the new young rector's frightened of heights,
So we don't even get a flag flown now on the greatest festivals.

But, as the sun rises on Mayday, and the Spring really starts,
    The cows still turn their heads to listen,
    And the horses still twitch their ears and shake out their manes,
        And the hens still cluck, very softly, and shift on last night's eggs,
    To hear the first shoots rustle from the soil,
        As creation begins again.

Creation

Before the first sparrow chirruped,
Everything must have been silent, still;
And the stiff, hard ridge of the skyline hills,
Terrified to speak even through the wind,
Asked nothing of the world.
Then, the sparrow spoke.
Everyone heard it, and loved it.
Pensive before, the trees shook themselves
And bowed to caress the grass.
Under its cover and protection,
Lithe worms processed through their tunnels,
In and out of the roots and bulbs.
Never before had mutual love so quickly spread,
And extended, between soil and plant and everything.

Abandoned

Stones stand here, roughly piled.
A short spire crowns the heap.
Glass, coloured, broken, lies beneath gapped teeth of fallen walls.
Within, the floor is puddled by the only-entrant rain,
Reflecting slateless beams, de-leaded now.
All is abandoned, lightless, derelict.

Next neighbour, now converted, proudly stands
In a neat garden. Father, tee-shirt and jeans,
Shows off the kitchen-apse, nave-sitting room
For cats on laps, his sanctuary-den,
And, from the bedroomed balcony on high,
Music beats out a modern kind of love.

What have we done, or rather failed to do,
That faith, told out no longer, seems to die?
Buildings put up for glory, gratitude,
No longer needed, insupportable,
Like leaders' promises, can be ignored
When no-one heeds their symbols or their cry.

Are there no corners where a candle still
Might burn a beacon for the coming day?
Our Source, His Name and Glory, go unheard
Where relevance determines when we fight.
Inevitable, when so few might ask, atuned elsewhere,
"What more than this should fill a fruitful day?"

Cathedral Close

Under the fearful man who ruled our life
Morning and evening, ruffs, and cassocks red
And, once accepted, surplice gleaming white.
"You sing for God," he said. "He hears each note,
Deserves naught but your best in pitch and tone and timing.
Count, boy, count!" And so we learnt
Disciplines and respect we never would forget.

And now, a man, retired, put out to grass,
I never thought I would return. And yet,
This place is haunting, haunted. Here are ghosts
Who shaped the person that I have become.
The towers and spires, the vaulting pillars, rise
Above the now-converted Canonry,
Protected by the western gate and ranges,
Cloister walls built to protect monks' peace
      Millennia ago.

And here I'll stay, one of the several men
Who could not stay away, and, every day,
Sit in a stall, above, behind the choir,
Hearing the settings which we used to sing,
And singing them again in heart and mind.

The Last Task

If we were born for a purpose,
Life is a series of tasks.
Since we are not born alone in this world,
We were born for the tasks to be service.
Life is a set of responsibilities
To be fulfilled for those around us.
We are the last to be bothered
About our comfort and ourselves.
That will be covered by others
Playing their parts.

Is this how it is?

And what of the last task each faces,
The task of dying? Undeniably,
We will all be required to do that,
And to do it responsibly, with care
For those whose service to us at that time
Will be to ease our way, as we must theirs,
As they swallow their tears and their fears
For themselves and the service they offer.

Our part of the task is simple: to go,
Leaving them to their grief and recovery
And service to those who remain.
Can we offer this courage, in fulfilment
Of why we were born? Pray we can.

Funeral, And Beyond

Dead in casket, soon to be laid in earth
Or rendered dust in unseen, hidden flames
Behind a curtain.

"Thanksgiving for the life of ..." Is that all
We are to be offered, when so few have touched
The lives of more than family and close friends?
Yes, those touches did change lives – a bit.
Few more than in the duties that we all
Owe to one another whom we meet
In the society of these crowded lives.
For their fulfilment of those duties – yes,
We should give thanks. But who is there
To hear us? Should our thanks not go
To them while they're alive and breathe and hear,
And know the love that thanks purport to offer?

And, curtains closed, and organ's gentle song,
Or screeching wail of diva, sending out
All those who came to say "Goodbye", "The End",
Who are there left who know it is "Adieu",
Who know goodbye is final, but who hope -
Who trust, who KNOW, that earthly death in fact
Is like a door, a gate, a portal, bridge
Into another land, where all the dead will live?

And who or what will live? The body we have burnt,
Or worms have spread through the rich soil of graveyard?
God Himself may, by a miracle, raise those bodies whole
At the Last Day; but what is clearer far
Is that, until that Day, our souls will live
In that great land, building the love taught there
On love learned hard here in our earthy life.

That is the job of soul – to live in LOVE,
The love of Servant-Saviour, love we can't
Completely practice in our lives down here
Where fears for Me, and selfishness, and pride
Distract us, and our conscious mind destroys
Determination to do better, yet again.
But once in Heaven, then our souls complete
What they can only start in earthly days.
This life, with all its starts and stops and pauses,
Reverses, pains and loss, cannot be all
The reason life was given to this Earth.
There must be more. There must be life beyond.
There must be Heaven.
In which case, let a funeral be joy,
The joy with which we wave off brides and grooms
To honeymoons, to everlasting love,
To future!
Leave the past's work rest, foundations
For a greater life to come.

And Next ..?

How do you live with insecurity?
      Hatred flies aircraft to collapse towers,
      Parks cars to build exploded headlines,
      Trains stopped, shops closed, a fearful walk to work,
      Violence, want –
But water, food, knowledge of beyond?

Not so in open savannah,
      Closed jungle,
      Dry earth unending,
      Continuous want,
      The edge of living.

Not so in barbed wired, burnt out
      Palm, clay, canvas,
      Blanketless camp
      For each succeeding generation.

Do you know insecurity? Not like theirs.
Pray God enough of us may keep the faith
      And prevent worse.

Index Of Titles

	Page
Abandoned	113
Aleppo, 2016	32
And Next … ?	118
And the Cars Went By	92
At the Marriage of …	25
Autumn	54
Beached People	26
The Bear's Spring	51
Bought At The Sales	81
Buttons	48
Caravaggio	60
Cat, Dreaming	77
Cathedral Close	114
Caught in the Hills	5
A Childhood Garden in Kent	30
Christmas, Here and Now	94
Coincidences	96
The Cottage By The Golf Course	22
Councillor Carter	41
Creation	112
Diver	104
Doubt and Faith	99
Eight Stones	110
The Engineer And The Poet	65

The English Mystery	70
The Expert	56
Fatherhood	89
Fireworks	28
Flamenco	9
Funeral, and Beyond	116
Gabble-Gobble	82
Heritage	53
In Pusscat's Power	86
Interior Decoration	21
Into Care	31
Khrushchev's Shoe	64
The Last Task	115
Lidded Pots	105
Love Is Not Everything	58
Many Reluctant Returns	17
Martyred by Lions	68
Merton	108
Midnight Sparrow	89
Moving House	44
Mr. Hughes' Removal Van.	20
My Grandpa's Beard	47
Nefusa, 1967	13
Next Door	59
No "Click-and-Drop" For Me	57

The Old Toby-Jug Maker	37
Overture and Beginners	8
Owl	84
Prejudices and Realities	80
Questions	98
Red Flares	3
Rembrandt	39
Ritual: Pen Hill	7
School Matinee	12
Sealers	23
Sequential Life	19
The Solution Was There All the Time	100
Sonnet of New Life	78
Sonnet to an Old-Fashioned Librarian	24
Spring in a Winter Place	61
Steps	79
Sunday	106
Sunny	75
Sunrise, on May-Morning	111
Sun, Shade and Cyclamen	11
That Hand at Table	29
To a Monastery Guesthouse	107
Valentine for a Long-Standing Relationship	63
Victim's Possessions	69
Views Across the Tyne	50
Violets	6
The Visiting Dragon	76

Wakefulness	103
Weekend Neighbours	55
Welsh Row, Beam Street	49
What Does She Do?	45
What Do You Make?	66
Where Is It, and What Is It For?	102
Working From Home	43
You Are The Other	97

Index Of First Lines

	Page
A hundred miles south from Tarabulus,	13
A night-walk on the limestone hills,	5
BANG! bang, bang, BANG! Whoosh, kerflub, kerflub, kerflub. "Aaaaarrh!"	28
Before the first sparrow chirruped,	112
Big and black and shaggy – that's the car.	51
Black cats come from London.	80
"Can you see her? Can you see her?"	25
Cat sleeps, curled, nose buried, whiskers bent,	77
Close to the grass-tops,	84
"Come up here and help me", she commands from the second floor landing.	43
Crystals and diet and numerology,	100
Dark, dark, the windows shuttered,	60
Darkness in here by seven,	89
Dead in casket, soon to be laid in earth	116
Diver,	104
"Don't you sit there, son!" he warned me,	41
Fatter, fatter, fatter grow the flanks of the shy deer	78
God gave an example; it's never enough.	106
Grubby little black ships, greasy-prowed, and chipped	23
He comes in the night, growling through the dark.	76

He looked from his small bedroom window	92
Here I am. Youthful. Even a confident smile,	39
Here on a bare beach, puffing	26
"He's here, he's here." "What, now?" "Yes,	20
How do you live with insecurity?	118
If Christ were born on Christmas night today,	94
If I were not a man, I'd be a gull,	79
If we were born for a purpose,	115
I glimpsed you through the nine-one-oh's,	24
"I got it at the sales, of course,	81
"I'm only a horny-handed, dirty-nailed engineer," you said,	65
I'm told – I can't remember - as a child,	30
In pitch darkness, we groped for a seat,	9
Inside the case of my Grandfather's grandfather clock,	17
In Spring, we watched them, bare but hazy green	19
In the midst of the Visitors' Parking, he sits and washes, 'till they've stopped	75
I saw you at the Village Hall,	63
I shall not ever see these things again.	31
I should not have come back!	32
It was a ritual, nothing more than that,	7
"I've oiled and put away the bat long since", he said to me.	54
Joseph doubted Her virginity.	99
Like ancient armies gathering for battle,	12
Love is not everything,	58
My Dad could read a football match – he said!	56
My Grandma had a button box,	48
My Grandpa's beard is bushy now,	47
My nearest neighbour, Mrs. Rowse,	59

Nikita Khrushchev was angry!	64
Oh, we're experts in our jobs. No two years are the same.	44
One afternoon in Spring, O best beloved,	6
One thing I'll never understand	70
On paper, the details were perfect,	22
Opposite the Cathedral, beneath the Giralda tower,	11
Orange sand. Evenly grained, flat as a tablecloth,	110
Over the holystoned step, bright whitened every day,	49
Partial poverty. Low, narrow streets. Drab back-to-backs.	50
See that church tower? They used to sing from there	111
She sits and watches from the dresser shelf	86
Silently, separately, when I first came,	107
Sleep. Sleep. Oh, for the gift of sleep!	103
So many broken heads and hearts,	68
Stage dark and theatre still, strings set the theme.	8
Stones stand here, roughly piled.	113
Submerged beneath molasses, there they float,	105
The fingers that I touched were long, and slim, and cool, and white,	29
The last policeman hoists his sodden hands	69
This is not where they sat, my forebears,	53
Through a birch-wood, in the morning sun	108
Tom Turkey went to London,	82
Under the fearful man who ruled our life	114
Warmth, in the day if not at night,	61
We are not yet machines.	102
We had a dark-blue kitchen wall at one time.	21

Well, I'm a teacher. I make lives, you see,	66
We sit along the water's edge,	55
What does she do in an evening?	45
What I remember most are those strong grey thumbs,	37
Wheee! It's ME! Standing in the prow,	57
White sails when they left, all those months ago,	3
Why was that beggar in that place at that time?	96
You are the Other.	97
You asked, "Do you believe in…"	98
You must have been terrified, Joseph,	89

Printed in Great Britain
by Amazon